Denis,

Your Journal
Starts Now!

ORGANIZATION CULTURE KILLERS

HOW LEADERS BUILD CULTURES OF SUCCESS

DEADLY

EXPECTATIONS

1

T.A. LASER

TAL PUBLISHING, LLC

Organization Culture Killers: Deadly Expectations 1

Portfolio/ TAL
An imprint of TAL Publishing, LLC
6725 South Fry Road; Suite 700 #345; Katy, TX 77494

Additional copies of this book can be ordered directly from the publisher at https://www.talaser.com, online (e.g.: Amazon.com, IngramSpark.com, etc.), and wherever else copies of this book are sold.

Contact T.A. Laser at:
https://www.talaser.com

Names: Tabitha A. Laser, Author.
Title: Organization Culture Killers: Deadly Expectations 1 / T.A. Laser.
Description: Texas: Portfolio / TAL, [2019]
ISBN 978-1-7328299-1-6 (hardcover)
ISBN 978-1-7328299-0-9 (paperback)
ISBN 978-1-7328299-2-3 (epub)

Subjects: Leadership | Success | Culture | Human Behavior | Organizational Learning | Risk Management | Business Management | Business Planning

Contents

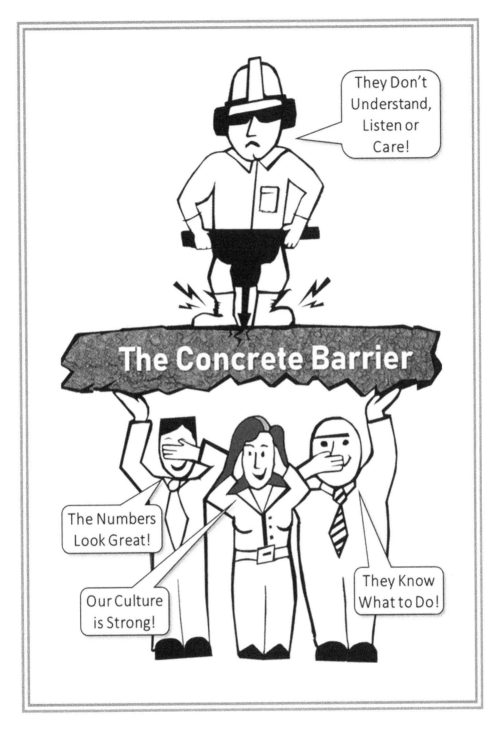

Try as they might, leadership simply could not figure out why their organization was performing so poorly.

For My Father,

Who taught me I could do anything and be anyone I wanted to if I put forth the effort, learned from my mistakes and treated others with kindness and respect.

The Journey

"You can be sure that whatever obstacles you are facing, others have faced similar things and have come through them, and you will face much bigger obstacles in the future. Recognize what is in your control and do something about it. Recognize what is outside your control and work around it."

— Alan Sugar

Before we get started, let's do a quick sense check.

1. Are you currently, or do you aspire to be, a business owner, board member, executive, leader, manager, supervisor, chairperson, figurehead, parent or person who inspires others to succeed?

2. Are you, or do you hope to be, responsible for the entire organization, territory, site, department, committee, group, association, community or household?

3. Have you ever struggled with growth, change, data overload, time management, prioritization, incidents, stress, finances, customer satisfaction, buy-in, resourcing, poor performance or quality, insubordination, compliance, maintaining balance, loyalty, retention or sustainability?

4. Do you wish life and work could be easier, safer, more profitable and more enjoyable?

If you answer yes to any of the previous questions, and you would like to quickly gain valuable career-advancing leadership knowledge and tools it took other leaders' decades to learn, then you've picked up the right book!

Lessons learned the hard way enable future leaders to succeed the easier way!

Organization Culture Killers by T.A. Laser exposes the Deadly Practices (DP) consuming valuable time and resources of businesses, governments and many more around the globe! These Deadly Practices are the practices organizations implement to improve performance, which end up backfiring, destroying their ability to succeed right under leadership's noses.

The Deadly Practices series consolidates learnings, solutions and guidance from organizations, leaders and experts around the globe into a timeless and non-judgmental collection of tools essential for success.

To survive and thrive, organizations must build more effective and sustainable pathways to success!

T.A. Laser is an insider with over 25 years of leadership experience and learnings. Throughout her life, Tabitha has had the great fortune to be mentored by many exceptional leaders and experience what "good looks like" and survive exposures to numerous Deadly Practices. She uses these experiences and learnings, in combination with her expertise in human behavior, leadership and risk reduction to help organizations reduce risks, strengthen cultures, improve performance and increase resiliency.

Anyone questioning Laser's credentials are sure to be pleasantly surprised by her extensive professional network, ethical prowess and impressive resume. Simply search for her on the internet of things, peruse her social media profiles, attend one of her keynote presentations or workshops, or chat with one of the thousands of people she has led, mentored, educated, coached, collaborated with and inspired.

A seasoned advisor to leaders at all levels and types of various-sized public, private and nonprofit organizations, Laser utilizes her insider access to reveal common observations, secrets and weaknesses, delivering eye-opening perspectives on why organizations continue to die along with innovative, life-saving methods.

Organizations continue to make decisions, often with the best intentions, that end up killing their culture, negatively impacting performance, and ultimately destroying their ability to succeed. Laser has coined these destructive decisions as "Deadly Practices."

In an age of big data, one would think organizations would be surviving and thriving, but Laser believes the opposite is occurring. She's noticed a dramatic increase in Deadly Practices over the past fifteen years, leaving the charred ruins of one organization after another in their wake.

She associates this recent decline to a global shortage of competent leaders due to inadequate mentoring opportunities and insufficient leadership development options. The younger generations are joining the workforce full of confidence, unwilling to put up with nonsense and prepared to jump at better opportunities if they arise. This is far different from the don't rock the boat, climb the ladder and work for the same organization until you retire or die mentality of more seasoned professionals.

With the ever-increasing emphasis on teaching to the test, decreasing attention spans, skyrocketing education costs, migration to independent online learning and everyone gets a trophy mentality, Laser believes the need for leadership development is greater now than ever before.

Unfortunately, existing leadership development options tend to focus more on management skills and task mastery, while options available to help develop strong leadership skills seem to be in short supply. Online programs are excellent knowledge stores, but Laser's concerns are that they fall short in developing personal and professional skills needed to be a strong leader. In addition, younger professionals entering the workforce miss out on valuable life lessons when they don't stay in one place long enough to learn from others, work through conflicts, or experience the euphoria from rising out of the ashes of failure.

Laser motivates and inspires readers to join her on a journey towards building cultures of success by sharing learnings, solutions and guidance from organizations, leaders and experts around the globe in this fun-to-read and timeless collection of leadership essentials.

Why learn the hard way when you can let someone else do it for you?

Readers will find themselves immersed in thought and unable to stop reading Laser's refreshing perspectives on success. Laser's nonjudgmental and relatable personality lures readers into a private tour of her topsy-turvy life, inspiring even the most obstinate to become stronger by looking for cracks of opportunity in their own reflection.

Don't be surprised when you find yourself nodding in agreement, clenching your fists in mutual frustration, laughing out loud at the ridiculousness and applauding when the pieces of the puzzle come together.

Learn how to improve your profitability and culture substantially while saving time and money, by eliminating deadly practices before it's too late!

The Deadly Practices Series

The intent of this series is to prevent repeating the mistakes of yesterday by educating, motivating and empowering the leaders of tomorrow with valuable knowledge, resources and tools for success. In short, the series is designed to be every educated leader's toolbox.

Sure, there are hundreds, if not thousands, of books on success, culture and leadership on the market, but who has time to read them all nowadays? Plus, as Phil Rosenzweig discusses in "The Halo Effect and the Eight Other Business Delusions that Deceive Managers", many of them have been written based on delusions

The experiences, learnings and eradication methods discussed in this series are universal and represent learnings from various leaders and industries around the world. They can be applied across the world, at work or home, and to any organization made up of two or more people.

In addition, Deadly Practices don't care who you are or what you do. Regardless if you are an owner of a global business, a shop floor supervisor, the chair of your neighborhood association or a college student with aspirations of greatness, this series will help you:

- ☐ Avoid common pitfalls, saving valuable time and resources
- ☐ Identify opportunities for personal and professional growth
- ☐ Build cultures of success
- ☐ Impact positive change through balanced decisions
- ☐ Inspire others to begin building better paths to success

Let's take a moment to discuss the title of the series since it has stirred up so many discussions. What is culture, and how can you kill it?

CULTURE

An integrated pattern of human knowledge, beliefs, and behaviors.

In other words, the way people do things around here!

The truth is that "Culture" is always present, no matter what we do to it, so you really cannot "Kill" it. With that being said, the type of Culture ultimately determines how successful performance will be, so I considered titling the books "Success Killers" and "Performance Killers" before finally landing on "Culture Killers." I chose "Culture Killers" because so many organizations are beginning to blame their poor performance on their workplace cultures without fully understanding what that really means. Hopefully, the "Culture Killers" title will encourage healthy discussions around what a workplace culture is and what factors actually lead to poor performance. Only then will we be able to address the source of the problem and impact sustainable positive change.

There are a few reasons I chose to title this series "Deadly Practices." First, I'm a huge horror fan! Books, movies, Halloween, etc. I consider horror-related materials as opportunities to learn what not to do. Like, don't go for a walk alone in a place you're not familiar with, especially if creepy music is playing.

Much like the learnings from scary movies, this series is based on my actual experiences and learnings along with those others have shared with me along my journey. I strongly believe that sharing these learnings with you will help you prevent repeating the mistakes of others and begin building better paths to success.

Also, this series is geared at raising awareness to efforts that many organizations implement and encourage, which are likely to backfire, causing unrepairable damage and catastrophic failure (AKA: Deadly Practices). Much of what is discussed in this series isn't new, and you have likely suffered through many of the same painful experiences as I have. The problem I am trying to solve with the series is providing a set of guides, a leadership toolbox if you'd prefer, that consolidates learnings and recommendations in an easy-to-read format. My hopes are that my style will resonate with young leaders, providing them with tools they may never learn. We all have so much to share, but tend to defend our turfs and attack anyone who could be a threat. I hope my efforts to tear or blow a hole in the Concrete Barrier (more on that later) will serve as a call to action for those praying for something better.

I've been asked to provide a formula for how many Deadly Practices it would take to cause an organization to fail. We love to stick numbers and percentages to everything, but the truth is, allowing even one deadly practice to wreak havoc on your organization can lead to destruction. With that said, your odds of failure will increase as the number of Deadly Practices increase, becoming exponentially more destructive when they play off of each other. Ultimately, failure depends heavily on the pain tolerance of your organization and stakeholders.

Since the intent of this series is to reveal Deadly Practices and solutions to help you impact positive changes in the future, I have purposely chosen not to include names of organizations or people in the books. In addition to some of the information coming from confidential sources, I also do not want to single anyone out as good or bad. Especially since so many organizations struggle with the same Deadly Practices, placing blame on one for the struggles of many is pointless.

Instead of comparing yourself to others, try to visualize each situation as if it were occurring in your organization. This internal reflection will increase your ability to identify threats to your organization, prioritize actions to address the issues and foster long-term success.

In an effort to keep things simple and avoid slowing down your read with soon-to-be-outdated information, I've opted to leave it out. Instead, additional information, recommended reads, templates, tools, and resources related to this series are maintained and available for your review/use online at www.talaser.com.

Sticking this book on a shelf to gather dust would be a tragedy. Instead, I encourage you to:

Apply what you learn towards impacting positive changes throughout your organization, community and personal life.

Deadly Expectations 1

This book is only a small piece of the bigger puzzle and simply the first of many steps along Tabitha's journey towards eradicating Deadly Practices and building better paths to success for the benefit of future generations.

The Organization Culture Killers Deadly Expectations book set centers around the Deadly Practices that wreak havoc on an organization's ability to succeed when leaders don't define, implement, deliver and change expectations thoughtfully. In an effort to keep things simple, the set has been broken out into the following four phases:

Deadly Expectations Book Set

Phase 1 - Build

Phase 2 - Ingrain

Phase 3 - Deliver

Phase 4 – Sustain

Deadly Expectations 1 is the first book in the Deadly Practices Series because it deals with foundational expectations upon which organizations are built. When building a house, you start by selecting a location, preparing the land, and then pouring the foundation before erecting the walls. Much like building a house, an organization should start by laying the groundwork for a strong foundation.

The Deadly Practices related to defining expectations are at the root of most of the cultural challenges facing organizations today. We will explore the disconnects caused between an organization's foundation for success and its culture of success when Deadly Expectations are present, and review solutions you can integrate into your existing systems to eliminate and prevent these Deadly Practices from leading your organization down the path to destruction.

In moving through the chapters, we'll examine and explain how many widely used Deadly Practices may be secretly undermining your organization's culture, efficiency, and effectiveness.

The most common terms and acronyms are included in the Definitions and Acronyms section at the back of the book for your reference.

Supercalifragilistic
-expialidocious

Now that I have your attention, let me draw your attention to the most important section in this entire book: the blank "Reflections and Commitments" pages (105-114) at the back of the book.

Go ahead, flip to them now, stick a tape flag on the first page to make it easier to access later. This book is merely a collection of a bunch of words and pictures. The true value will come from what you do with the words!

Take time to jot down your personal reflections and the commitments you would like to implement in your organization and/or personal life to begin building a better path to success.

Once done, simply rip out your notes and add them to your to-do-list, or delegate them to someone else.

Your Journey to Building a Better Path to Success Begins Now!

Introduction

"The path to destruction is often
paved with best practices and
good intentions."

T.A. Laser

Deadly Practices aren't new. They are an age-old problem that just keep repeating. For centuries, they've plagued and weakened public, private and nonprofit organizations of all sizes across the globe. You name the organization, and it will likely have a sad tale to tell about tangling with Deadly Practices.

Let's take a quick look at two such instances in very different organizational realms and worlds.

The Two-Faced Monarch

During his reign from 1865 to 1909, Belgium's King Leopold II came to be known as the "Builder King." He was an influential and activist monarch who advocated strongly for his people. Under his leadership, Belgians became more prosperous and safer than they'd been in generations. Leopold advocated for pro-labor reforms and even granted workers the right to strike. Beyond that he set in place egalitarian protections for women and children, including outlawing child labor. Not exactly the norm in the 19th century. He used infrastructure projects to stimulate employment and economic growth, much like Franklin Delano Roosevelt would in the United States more than 100 years later. Leopold was a domestic visionary and a progressive leader for the times.

Yet he's mostly remembered for the atrocities of the Congo. Unlike in Belgium, there was no political infrastructure in place in the Congo where Leopold also ruled, though in absentia. Without checks and balances in place, Leopold made a fortune extracting ivory and later processing rubber from the region using slave labor. Belgium needed capital, and the Congo had valuable resources. He put a Congolese police force in power to govern in his absence. There was little end to the levels of violence and brutality used by that force. Ultimately, history estimates that as many as 10 million people were killed in Africa during Leopold's pursuit to expand Belgian's wealth. The rights and protections Leopold's people enjoyed domestically were completely absent abroad.

How could one leader simultaneously be a progressive savior in one location and a monster in another? Deadly Practices. By failing to have a consistent system of expectations in place across all the territories he was responsible for managing, Leopold's rule in the Congo lapsed into brutality, leaving him as a sad footnote and case study in the awful history of colonization. Imagine if he had governed the Congo as he had governed Belgium: boldly, progressively, and fairly.

If Leopold had been able to identify and correct the Deadly Practices we'll be talking about in this book, he quite possibly could have bridged the gap between the way his policies at home were implemented and carried out and his policies abroad were employed. Imagine if the incompetent government ruling the Congo in his absence had been held to standards of responsibility and accountability. Imagine the loss of lives that might have been avoided had consequences been enforced and direct oversight from the C-Suite (Leopold himself in this instance) used.

When Deadly Practices are left unchecked, we too often see history leading to heartbreak.

The Demise of a Darling

In 1985, a merger was finalized between two companies: Houston Natural Gas, and InterNorth Inc. of Omaha. Enron was born. The new company and its now infamous tipped-E logo quickly set about rebranding into an energy company that quickly benefited from an era of energy deregulation and the growing dot-com bubble.

Between 1996 and 2001, Fortune named Enron "America's Most Innovative Company" six years in a row. Enron wasn't just on top of the tech market, they owned the whole Fortune 500 show.

In October of 1999, Enron created Enron Online, an electronic trading website that made Enron counterparty to every transaction. Not surprisingly, many were buying Enron stock at the time. Suddenly Enron, in one shape or form, was either a buyer or a seller in every transaction. They were making a fortune. At its height, Enron's brilliant trading platform was executing $350 billion in trades annually. When the dot-com bubble began to burst, Enron invested hundreds of millions of dollars into broadband networks that realized almost no returns instead of protecting its positions. By the recession of 2000, Enron was exposed across the most volatile parts of the market. Yet its stock price had reached an all-time high of $90.56.

What happened in the next two years was a stunning fall from grace, and a case study in the danger of compounding Deadly Practices.

As Enron watched its market capitalization decrease, the company started hiding financial losses using mark-to-market accounting, a technique where you value a security based on its current market value instead of its actual book value. While this can work well for trading securities which fluctuate in real value, it's disastrous for actual businesses. This questionable accounting practice was signed off on by reputable accounting firms and auditors, even as Enron continued to disguise its growing losses. When the company stock failed to keep appreciating as executives had anticipated, which would have pulled the company's actual value back up to its inflated perceived value, the losses became overwhelming and irrecoverable.

In October 2001, Enron reported a $618 million quarterly loss. By December, Enron had declared bankruptcy, the largest in U.S. history. The next month criminal investigations were launched. Two weeks later the once-Wall Street darling and its valueless stock were removed from the NYSE.

Nobody purposely sets out to implement Deadly Practices into their organizational culture.   Often these practices are implemented inadvertently with the best of intentions. Consider King Leopold, who may initially have set out to make money in the Congo to fund progressive reforms back in Belgium. Consider Enron, the hot stock that hid from the financial reality of shifting markets in the hopes of staying on top.

It's obvious with Enron and King Leopold that not everyone in the organization was operating under the same plan. Had they had this book or a plan at all to define, communicate, enforce, and deliver on expectations, things may have gone differently.

After centuries, Deadly Practices remain a major problem infiltrating organizations at an alarming and increasing rate. If left unchecked in organizations, they can be Organization Culture Killers, reducing an established Fortune 500 company or even an entire government into a pile of smoking, well-intentioned ruins.

A Time for Action

If you look deeply, you'll find many overlapping Deadly Practices between King Leopold and Enron. Of course, they're not alone in their missteps. Sadly, Deadly Practices exist in some degree, in nearly every organization across the globe.

These disasters could have easily been avoided. There's no excuse for letting Deadly Practices destroy your organization. This series highlights learnings from multiple organizations and reveals proven solutions you can implement to avoid a similar fate.

First, the existence of Deadly Practices must be acknowledged. In our era of renewed social responsibility among all organizations, it's time to become our best and most responsible selves at the individual, institutional, and global level. With economies constantly in a state of crisis, organizations failing daily, governmental coups, international strife, plummeting loyalty on the parts of employers and employees alike, and a plethora of other problems plaguing organizations around the world, one must wonder, why do we keep making the same mistakes again and again?

This may be a difficult pill for some to swallow, but I believe many of our problems can be fixed if we just look in the mirror. No, not to check out our awesome hairdo or to see if we have food in our teeth. I'm talking about having the courage to see our own weaknesses in the mirror and strive to find ways we can personally make a difference. This isn't easy to do. It may seem impossible at times, but it is necessary if we want to impact positive change. Pointing fingers and blaming others will get us nowhere.

Second, we need to eradicate the Deadly Practices in our personal and professional lives and implement measures to prevent them from occurring to create a more resilient and stable future.

So, where's the best place to start?

Well, at the beginning, of course! We need to start with Deadly Expectations because they lie at the root of all problems. To put it another way, an organization's failure to get its expectations right will make it virtually impossible to eradicate any of the other Deadly Practices.

If an organization's culture does not align with its expectations, the consequences can be catastrophic. This applies to large organizations, start-ups, and even newlyweds. If we take this opportunity to look in the mirror, we'll see that it's impossible for a culture of success to exist if we don't take the necessary steps to build, ingrain, deliver and sustain our expectations for success first. Performance will suffer, success will be fleeting or remain out of reach, and one day the organization will collapse if the Deadly Expectations revealed in this book are ignored.

Do you know how many Deadly Practices have wreaked havoc on your organization in the past, and how many are currently causing destruction right under your nose?

Simply watch the news, skim the paper, peruse the internet, check out social media, or go old-school and read a history book to see evidence of the devastation caused by Deadly Practices.

It's time to stop repeating history and start controlling our destiny!

Here's the great news! This book reveals the Deadly Practices associated with building your foundation, what to watch out for and methods to eliminate and prevent them from jeopardizing your organization's ability to survive and thrive.

Once your mind is conditioned to recognize Deadly Practices, you'll never have to fall victim to them again!

The Path to Success

"Have no fear of the future. Let us go forward into its mysteries, tear away the veils which hide it from our eyes, and move onwards with confidence and courage."

Winston Churchill

Leaders constantly claim that their management system is "good enough" or that they don't need a management system because their organization hasn't grown large enough yet. It doesn't matter if you are an organization of two people or two million, building a strong foundation is necessary for every organization to grow rapidly, survive market shifts and achieve sustainable success.

I recently consulted for a very small organization comprised of eight employees. The owner told me about the previous organization he had owned, which rose to the top quickly and then fell apart to the point of collapse even faster.

Since then, he had decided to part ways with his previous partners and try again. Much like his previous organization, things appeared to be going well in the beginning, however history was starting to repeat itself. He told me the organization was struggling to perform because his employees weren't doing their jobs well, turnover was high, and things were falling through the cracks.

When I asked to see his management system, he just stared at me like a deer in headlights. When I explained what a management system was in terms he could understand, his response was to laugh and state that his organization was too small to waste time on things like a management system when growth was the priority. He was under the impression his employees were the problem, when his problems were actually rooted in his organization's failure to build a strong foundation.

Even the smallest organizations need a management system.

This is just one of many similar examples where small organizations built quickly on weak foundations find themselves on the unpleasant path to destruction over and over again.

Large organizations who don't define their foundation when they are small and then grow fast suffer the same fate. Enron could be a case study of a company that started smaller, grew quickly, and never fully defined its mission, vision, values, and management system. If they had, the company likely would have avoided its corrupt hires and shady practices.

So, what does the path to success look like? Image 1 illustrates an unobstructed path to success between the foundation for success built and ingrained by senior leadership, and the culture of success that delivers and sustains performance in alignment with the mission, vision, values and expectations defined in the foundation of an organization.

Building on a weak foundation may work for a while, depending on the organization's pain tolerance, but will ultimately cause even the mightiest of organizations to crumble when too much pressure is applied.

Unfortunately, organizations often mistakenly believe that their foundation is strong, or do not recognize the importance of building a foundation at all, only to learn about the erosive Deadly Practices undermining their efforts and weakening their ability to succeed after significant damage has been done. By the time they realize there are foundational problems, many organizations find themselves pouring excessive resources into repairing and reinforcing their foundations to support their ever-increasing weight of growth. This habit is not sustainable and is long overdue for an overhaul.

An organization must have a strong foundation of success upon which to build if they want to travel the path to success.

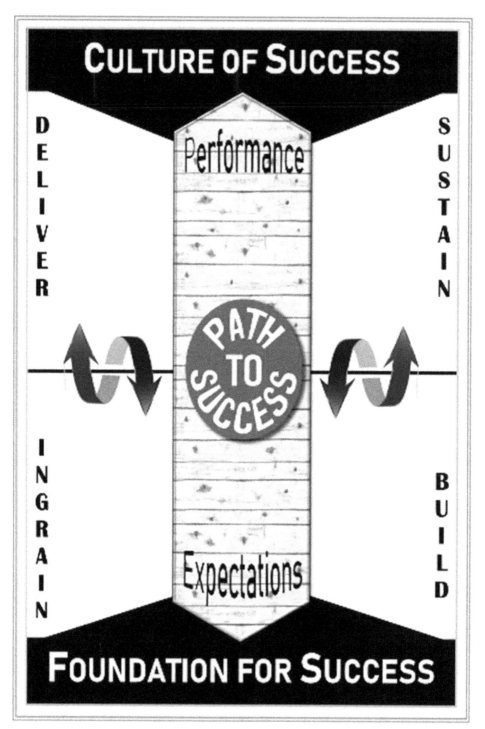

Image 1 – The Path to Success

22

The Concrete Barrier

If you dig deep enough to find the root cause of many Deadly Practices, you'll likely unearth a giant elephant lurking in your organization. The elephant I'm referring to is the "concrete barrier", which is the muse for the cartoon at the beginning of the book and illustrated in Image 2.

The concrete barrier is an invisible barrier to success that blocks and distorts the flow of information between senior leadership who defines success and the rest of the workforce expected to deliver success. The concrete barrier creates the following communication disconnects, which will be covered in more detail later. It enables Deadly Practices to multiply and spread throughout an organization without detection.

1. Fear ➔ No Information

2. Ignored/Misunderstood ➔ Partial Information

3. Incentivized to Lie ➔ False Information

I believe some form of concrete barrier is present in every organization. If you've experienced any of these three disconnects, your foundation has weaknesses that are putting your organization at risk.

The good news is that you now know it exists, and as G. I. Joe would say,

"knowing is half the battle".

Throughout the Deadly Expectations book set we will be discussing the Deadly Practices most responsible for the creation of concrete barriers, along with many methods other organizations have applied to eradicate them.

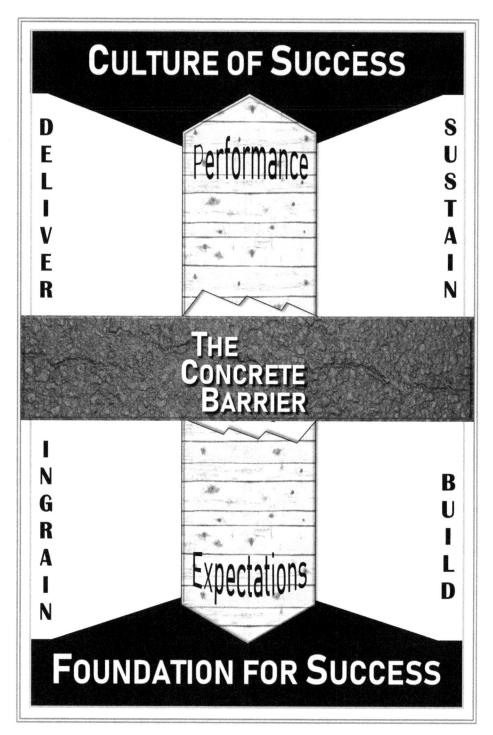

Image 2 -   The Concrete Barrier

DP 1

Undefined Expectations

"By failing to prepare, you are preparing to fail."

Benjamin Franklin

Have your kids ever pleaded ignorance when you asked them what they had for homework? I know mine have. I've found the issue isn't always them, but a lack of clearly communicated expectations or assignments.

Likewise, how can an organization ever expect consistent results and long-term success if it doesn't define expectations or show how those expectations lead to success?

The problem often isn't your kids, and neither is it your employees. The problem is that we rarely define our expectations clearly, whether at home or at work.

If an organization doesn't define what success looks like to them and the expectations necessary to be successful, then their culture is set up for catastrophe. Failure to define expectations is like trying to pour your organization's foundation over a pit of quicksand. Regardless of how great its leadership, employees, market and customers, the organization will ultimately be engulfed by the sands of indecision, conflicting priorities and inconsistency if there isn't a target to aim for.

Have you heard the saying, "Marching to the same drummer"? It's a term often used because a marching band that doesn't stay in rhythm will sound horrible. Well, an organization that does not clearly define its expectations would be equivalent to a marching band comprised of the best musicians in the world trying to follow multiple drummers with one playing the beat to Jingle Bells, one playing the National Anthem and the other playing Bohemian Rhapsody. It would be impossible for everyone to play in sync, regardless of how skilled they are, fine-tuned their instruments are or how great their band leader is, thus turning their beautiful notes into nauseating noise.

Image 3 illustrates how undefined expectations fail to penetrate the concrete barrier, preventing organizations from building a path to success.

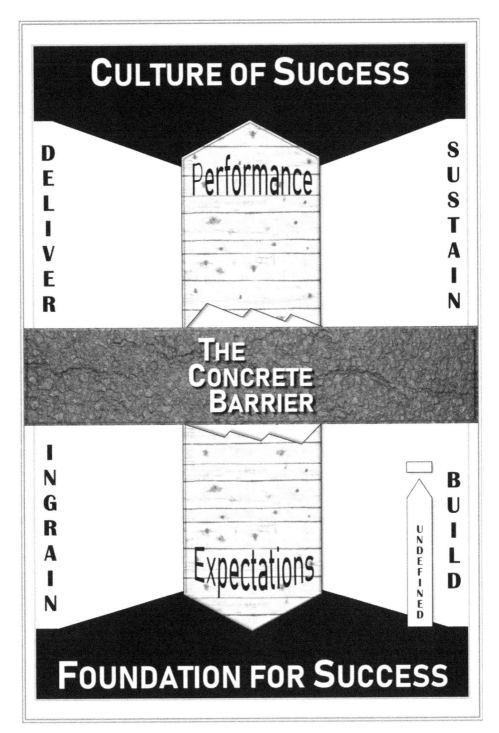

Image 3 – Undefined Expectations

27

This is why Undefined Expectations is the worst Deadly Practice an organization can fall victim to. Undefined Expectations will cause even the greatest organization to crumble like a sandcastle under an incoming tide unless its pain tolerance is high and market forgiving.

If you don't know what you want or how to get it, how is it ever going to get done?

Unfortunately, most organizations miss the mark when building their foundation because they don't take the time to clearly define what success looks like.

There are tons of books, articles, blogs and podcasts who tout having the secrets to success and how to be the best, but the truth is there is not one answer. Everyone is different and unique in some way, so what works for one may not work for the others. Depending on the type of organization and its leadership, success can be defined extremely differently, ranging from making money, to helping others, to hurting others (e.g.: terrorists).

Often, organizations will have a vague understanding of what they think success is, but don't go through the painful process to dig deep down and find out what they really want to be when they grow up. As human beings, we have egos, opinions and beliefs that do not always align; so whenever an organization is made up of more than one person it becomes more difficult to agree on the definition of success and easier for Deadly Practices to lead us down the path to destruction.

The scariest part of this deadly practice is that organizations rarely realize they have built their foundation on quicksand until they have already spent tremendous time and resources on growth. This is partially because they don't understand what a strong foundation is or what Deadly Practices to avoid. It isn't until problems start to arise that they recognize the weaknesses in their foundation. This is when organizations go into survival mode, merely adding insult to injury as they attempt to patch the cracks in

Blindly pursuing a path weakened by
deeply-rooted Deadly Practices can be fatal to your
organization's health.

their foundation with unthoughtful decisions and poorly executed quick fixes, instead of addressing the real root of their problems. Organizations need to go back to the drawing board and redesign their foundation to enable their organization to survive and thrive for the long run. Sometimes, taking a step backwards is the only way to move forwards. It may be painful at first, but the rewards for doing so can be limitless!

Culture of Ignorance

I've had the unfortunate privilege of working for and with dozens of organizations who have struggled to define their expectations in a manner that will lead to sustained success. Sadly, both my professional and personal life suffered each time I became trapped in chaotic downward spirals of devastation triggered by organizations allowing cultures of ignorance to fester.

Fortunately, as Mahatma Gandhi eloquently said, "from suffering comes enlightenment"!

It is because of my experiences, both good and bad, that I understand what works and what tends to backfire and am able to share the good stuff with you!

Demolished by Growth

I have worked for and with Fortune 500 companies, governments and with the smallest of start-ups, and experienced growth, decline and company acquisitions from both sides. During my career, I've conducted numerous culture and compliance assessments for organizations before, during and after mergers and acquisitions. Over and over again, I've found undefined expectations to be the most destructive to organizations that grow quickly and those going through mergers and acquisitions.

Introducing new leaders, employees and systems is often difficult and messy. What happens next, how does life look from here on, and what are the expectations of new employees are critical elements of the acquisition process. Sadly, they're often ignored or under-attended to as the focus falls on lagging indicators and performance instead of where it needs to be – the foundation.

The term "fake it until you make it" is used frequently. This can be true and a very valuable approach if you build upon a strong foundation. Walls can fall, and pipes may burst, but those can always be replaced if your foundation is solid.

Another common saying is, "We don't want to be too descriptive because that would hinder innovation." Innovation is amazing and necessary for growth, but if expectations aren't defined, then innovation can quickly turn into a bottomless pit of excessive spending, backstabbing and inefficiency. This may sound absurd, but a solid foundation includes processes for encouraging innovation constructively and effectively. Simply not defining or doing something is going to take you down the path to destruction, so if your organization falls in this group, Stop, Drop & Roll yourself back a step as soon as possible. Waiting even one more day could be disastrous!

The other opinion I come across frequently is "We don't define organization-wide expectations because there are too many differences (e.g.: geographic locations, business units, etc.)." Sure, there may be differences, but if we look in the mirror, every single person is different too.

Trying to appease everyone's differences by not defining your expectations for success would be like restaurant chains not having menus. Just imagine how hard it would be for a restaurant chain to negotiate lower prices with suppliers, maintain any resemblance of consistency between locations and prepare for every customer's demands when the meal options are infinite. Chaos is the word that pops into my head.

So, what can you do to prevent Undefined Expectations from destroying your organization?

You may be surprised, but the answer is to standardize, in a fit-for-purpose way of course! Much like a menu, organizations need to define consistent expectations across their portfolio that are flexible enough to account for differences when they exist without jeopardizing success.

I wouldn't expect a farm producing feedstock for biofuels to do everything the same as an off-shore refinery operating under the same parent organization.

What is necessary is for the parent organization to define its mission, vision and values and expectations in a way that can easily be interpreted by all, while including processes for granting flexibility to those where doing so does not make sense.

We need to stop demanding everyone do things the same, and start expecting everyone to align to our expectations for success. Note, align doesn't mean do things the same, it simply means "march to one drummer."

Eradication Methods

All it takes to eradicate the Undefined Expectations Deadly Practice is to take the time to define them! The tricky parts are knowing what to define and how to set aside egos long enough to get the job done.

Building a solid foundation is challenging to accomplish if you have already built your foundation on quicksand, but it can be extremely easy to do when you're just getting started. Unfortunately, many startups don't think they need to spend time building their foundation and suffer tremendously once they begin growing.

Which of the following paths will you take when you identify cracks in your organization's foundation? Choose wisely!

☐ **A.** Continue to throw quick fixes, over complication and unnecessary resources into reinforcing your weak foundation, hoping for a continuous miracle to save your organization from distinction.

☐ **B.** Cook your books and sell your organization to the next clueless investor who comes by, leaving senior leadership with fat pockets and devastation in your wake.

☐ **C.** Take a step back and build a strong foundation for sustainable success.

Even though history is filled with organizations who chose options A and B above, I'd personally choose option C.

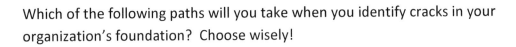

Don't wait until it's too late!

If you are one of the many organizations who have developed a strong foundation, then fantastic! Unfortunately, I have yet to encounter an organization whose expectations were strong. Many have had great parts and not-so-great parts, but none have been completely great.

After conducting numerous assessments and analyzing hundreds of failures, I believe organizations need to do a better job of defining what success looks like.

Define Success

Every organization needs to define what success means to them before a solid foundation can be built. Those who fail to articulate what success looks like risk ending up in a constant state of confusion, indecision and wastefulness.

Many organizations attempt to define success in their mission, vision, values and business plans. Unfortunately, most water theirs down with so much wordsmith hype and political correctness, that a great deal of room is left open for interpretation.

Dozens of the leaders and professionals I interviewed struggled to define what success meant to their organization. Sure, they could read, and sometimes quote from memory, their organization's mission, vision and values, but couldn't explain what it all meant. The most common reason for their confusion was leadership's never-ending reinterpretations of success.

Constant change, especially when done without thought and understanding of the potential risks, can be extremely harmful to the well-being of an organization.

I've noticed that organizations' definitions of success tend to change when there are senior leadership changes, increased shareholder pressures and knee-jerk reactions to internal and external events (e.g.: market shifts, accidents, etc.).

I believe part of the problem is the lack of guidelines for leadership to follow when defining success. When looking for proof, the stock market is a great place to start because share prices are merely a response to how organizations are performing against their definition of success. Some leaders do a much better job defining success, and by doing so maintain control of their future, while leaders who poorly define success become stock market puppets.

For many, the hardest part of defining success is identifying what factors to address. The following are some factors that should be addressed when defining success:

1. Domestic Factors
2. Global Factors
3. Supply and Demand
4. Interest Rates
5. Competitors
6. Earnings
7. Risk Profile
8. Workforce Competency
9. Trade Cycle
10. Speculation
11. Political Factors
12. Government Stability
13. Market Opinions
14. Institutional Investors
15. Foreign Investment
16. Available Credit
17. Regulatory Effectiveness
18. Social Impacts
19. Environmental Impacts
20. Workforce Culture
21. Quality
22. Customer Satisfaction

It's important to be smart when addressing these factors. And by smart, I mean your definition of success should include specific, measurable, achievable, relevant and time-bound plans related to each factor.

Taking the time to thoroughly define success is only the first step towards building a better path to success. It is also important to measure your organization's progress towards success. I've been working with professors and subject matter experts for years to develop a tool that will help organizations gain visibility to their progress along the path to success and am excited to share it with you in the next section.

Define Expectations

So, what's the best way to build a strong foundation, you may be wondering? You're in luck! I've been taking notes through the years and have built the framework for a system that will help any organization, new or established, build a strong foundation and eradicate this Deadly Practice. You can refer to it however you want, but I call it OPALS.

OPALS is the Operating and Performance All-Inclusive Leadership System.

OPALS

Operating and

Performance

All-Inclusive

Leadership

System

The best part, you don't have to pay me millions of dollars for OPALS! You're getting access to it just by reading my book. Awesome, eh?

OPALS combine the most important elements every organization needs to define from the top if they want to be successful and remain successful long into the future. The elements of OPALS are described below:

- # Expectations

  This element is where the organization defines what success looks like for them, and includes their mission, values, goals, objectives, plans, policies, organizational structure, employee engagement, accountability, etc.

- # Risk Management

  This element defines how the organization identifies and controls performance, people and public risks.

- # Competency

  This element defines the roles and responsibilities necessary to support the organization, along with the knowledge, skills and demonstrated abilities required to fill those roles.

- # Operating Standards

  This element defines the standards necessary for successful operations, including document control, management of change, contractor management, health and safety, environmental management, operating procedures, etc.

- # Performance Standards

  This element defines what performance is necessary for the organization to succeed, including market expectations, Key Performance Indicators (KPIs), quality control, customer satisfaction, marketing plan effectiveness, etc.

- # Resiliency

  This element is critical for organizations who want to reap the rewards from sustainable success. It includes emergency response planning and response, incident management, business continuity planning, public involvement, etc.

- ## Assurance

  Assurance is one of the top elements that organizations define poorly or fail to define altogether. This element includes behavior observations and conversations, preventative maintenance, assessments and inspections (Note: I believe audits need to be eliminated from our vocabulary, and will be expanding on that later in the series), data reporting and analysis, etc.

- ## Continuous Improvement

  This element is essential for organizations who want to prevent making continuous mistakes and stay ahead of their competition. It includes defining how the organization learns from internal and external sources, in addition to how it integrates the applicable learnings effectively.

- ## Deviations

  This is probably the most abused and/or neglected element. Often, when an organization defines their expectations for deviations, they either mean everyone has to follow everything verbatim or face the firing squad, or they stuck something in there because they were told they had to but usually just let everyone do whatever they want regardless. What many organizations do not realize is the importance of this element. It is like the glue that holds everything together. If defined correctly, it will ensure everyone stays in alignment with the organization's expectations, while still allowing appropriate flexibility for their workforce to perform excellently in different environments, climates and situations.

Getting everything done in order isn't important!

What is important is that you define the OPALS elements before this Deadly Practice has the opportunity to kill your culture and destroy your organization.

Now that you have a clearer view of what elements make up a strong foundation, what are you planning to do next?

Review the following recommended next steps, reflect on what your organization needs, and write down your commitments to impact positive changes on the blank Reflections and Commitments pages in the back of the book.

Next Steps

1. Ensure your organization has clearly defined what success looks like.

2. Download the OPALS checklist from www.talaser.com and go through it with a team comprised of leadership and the workforce to confirm you have defined everything necessary for sustainable success.

3. Conduct in-depth gap assessments (more on these later) to understand the effectiveness of your existing management system and identify potential weaknesses in your foundation.

4. Where gaps and inefficiencies are identified, develop a plan to bridge the gaps and document your organization's expectations for success.

5. When in doubt, reach out for help. Schedule a consultation with a qualified OPALS Executive Coach online at www.talaser.com for assistance building your OPALS or modifying your existing management system to align with the OPALS elements,

DP 2

Unclear Expectations

"There is nothing so useless as doing efficiently that which should not be done at all."

Peter Drucker

You've worked hard to build your OPALS. But what good is that beautiful, all-inclusive system if your expectations don't make any sense?

Far too often, organizations develop their management systems without much forethought, or with far too much complexity. It's an extremely difficult line to walk between too much and too little, but it's a line that needs to be walked if an organization wants to survive and thrive.

When an organization takes the time to define their expectations, but doesn't take the time to get them right, the concrete barrier rears its ugly head again. As illustrated in Image 4 by the arrow landing in the middle of the concrete barrier, unclear expectations make it to the workforce, but don't deliver success because they are missing important aspects necessary to get there. This disconnect between what leadership wants and how the workforce performs leads to a Culture of Confusion.

Culture of Confusion

When the expectations are not clear, it is extremely difficult for leadership to guide the organization down the path to success, and even more challenging for the workforce to understand and deliver successfully. A culture of confusion plagues organizations whose expectations   are   too vague or too complicated.

The secret to balance is finding the sweet spot!

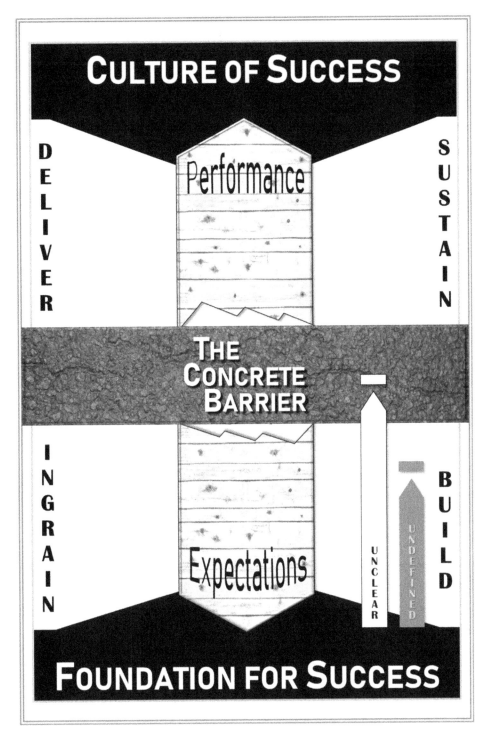

Image 4 - Unclear Expectations

43

Vague Expectations

Some organizations view the vagueness of their expectations positively, believing doing so leaves room for innovation and independent thought. It rarely surprises me to see these types of organizations grow extremely fast, only to crash back down to reality even faster. The main reason for this is because innovation and independence can easily derail an organization onto a path to destruction if a strong foundation isn't in place to support its constantly moving structure.

When expectations are too vague, the potential for fatal conflicts and catastrophic errors increases dramatically.

Conflicts arise when different people interpret unclear expectations in conflicting ways and their paths collide. One organization I worked for struggled a great deal with this problem. They had purposely left their management system vague enough that each site could remain independent. As mentioned earlier, when I start with an organization my priority is always to come up to speed with its expectations and culture. This situation was no different. The site I was responsible for quickly aligned with the organization's expectations and everything seemed to be going great. Then, the bottom dropped out from under us when the mother ship started sending out auditors. Our culture quickly took one hit after another as auditor after auditor appeared, each with completely different interpretations of conformance. We would be told to change something one week, only to be written up for not having it the way it used to be the next week. Our site leadership was doing its best to keep the sharks at bay and prevent the constantly changing instructions from destroying the positive culture we had fostered. Then, the organization decided to throw a Molotov cocktail our way when they transferred in a new leader who completely disagreed with most of the organization's expectations altogether. As I am sure you can imagine, chaos ensued, and as a result of organizational changes, that site is no longer in their portfolio.

The worst part of this situation was that the expectations were defined and had the potential to support the organization, but their decision to be vague led to world-wide conflicts, inefficiencies and errors that have since brought the once mighty giant to its knees. Yes, the organization is still around and can still right its sinking ship. The question is, will they take the steps necessary to do so, or will they keep ignoring the truth and blaming others for their mistakes? Only time will tell.

In addition to conflicts, errors increase when critical information is not included. Let's use baking as an example. There are a lot of recipes out there on the Internet of Things to choose from. Just because someone has taken the time to write down the recipe and snap a few photos doesn't mean what you attempt to duplicate will turn out tasting good.

A few years ago, I returned home from a business trip to Scotland determined to recreate the pavlova from one of my dinner meetings. After perusing the Internet of Things, I found a recipe and proceeded to follow it verbatim. To my dismay, my pavlova turned out to be a big pile of goopy nastiness! Why? Well, that's what I wanted to know too. I was so confused. The recipe listed all of the ingredients and I had followed the instructions meticulously. Only after coming across another recipe later did I learn that the eggs needed to be at room temperature first. The author made a critical mistake when they either forgot to mention it or assumed everyone knew this crucial egg tip, and

the omission ended up costing me resources, time and my pride.

Overcomplicated Expectations

On the other end of the spectrum, organizations tend to overcomplicate their expectations. This usually occurs when organizations try to make repairs to cracks in their foundation, are too prescriptive, or don't fully understand their risks.

Including too much information makes it hard for people to know what is really important. It also introduces the risk of conflicting directions and misinterpretation.

As demonstrated by the architect and furniture designer, Ludwig Mies Van Der Rohe, one of the founders of modern architecture and a proponent of simplicity of style, "Less is more."

By less I mean less complexity, not having less expectations.

Semantic complexity correlates with the number of ways meaning can be derived and interpreted from an utterance. It also is associated with the types of syntactical structures necessary for it to be an intelligible utterance, and the number of different pathways meaning can be retrieved from (how easy or difficult it is to prompt for recall).

A great example of over complication causing unclear expectations is the use of the term "Best Practices." Though used frequently, this term is a fallacy. If there were such things as best practices, then there wouldn't be room to improve, and we'd still believe the world is flat.

In an interesting online conversation, one professional criticized me for my LinkedIn article titled "Let's Build a Better Path to Success" (www.linkedin.com/pulse/lets-build-better-path-success-tabitha-a-laser-csp/) insinuating best practices are fluid, adaptive processes that will have measured rigidity and be allowed to continuously transmute.

In my experience, this is what best practices should be, however the term is misleading. We continue to use terms that don't say what they mean, requiring a secret decoder ring or an encyclopedia to define them. Unfortunately, I've witnessed many leaders interpret best practices to mean they are the best and therefore do not need additional time or resources invested on them to improve.

> "Best practices can quickly
> become our best prisons."
>
> — Jeffrey Dalto

Instead of saying best practices, wouldn't it make sense to call a spade a spade and call them what they really are? Some organizations have already made significant strides in simplifying things by changing best practices to best-for-now or better practices.

Another example is the term "Safety First." I've often stated that this term is a huge culture killer for many reasons, of which I'll elaborate on briefly.

Safety First? Not Really!

With the growing emphasis on workplace safety, you can imagine how well my view on this matter is received. No joke, I've actually had a manager spitting and cursing at me for disagreeing with his lifelong motto of "safety first". The only reason I'm sharing this embarrassing moment with you is because this type of reaction is normal when challenging someone to observe things from a different perspective.

Be honest, what is the very first thought that goes through your head when you see a sign or hear someone say, "Safety First"? I'm going to use my magic powers and predict you would think, "not 100% of the time" and do a figurative or literal eye roll. Am I close?

Interestingly enough, I observe similar reactions nearly every time someone says, "Safety First". This is because deep down in our subconscious we know safety is NOT first all of the time. If it were, we'd never drive a car, use public restrooms or go outdoors when it's raining. So, by saying something that isn't true, the subconscious of others peg us as liars and untrustworthy.

In addition, saying "Safety First", and then constantly putting workers in situations where other priorities trump safety becomes very confusing. Is safety first? Is it not? What is it, and why do I get blamed for it when it's convenient for the organization? And on, and on.

But wait, there's more! Not only are we lying when we say, "Safety First", confusing them when we don't always put safety first, but we are also enabling them to be dependent on others for their actions. I'll go into this in more detail later in the series but want to touch on it now to help you understand the seriousness of saying what you mean.

The whole shift to a culture of caring can be dangerous when taken out of context. For example, if "Safety First" means everyone should care about and constantly watch out for everyone else's safety, then personal accountability can easily get lost. I mean, why do I need to remember to put on my safety glasses when I know someone else will remind me if I forget? This may seem like a silly example, but the compilation of little silly things tends to cause the most damage.

Let's pull it all together. What we're left with after saying "Safety First" is a workforce full of untrusting, dependent risk takers. That's the exact opposite of the intention of saying "Safety First"! Bingo! As I've mentioned previously, the path to destruction is paved with good intentions.

If you are set on making safety a priority, then by all means, go for it. Now, answer honestly, do you believe safety is really, truly, first, all of the time? Sure, in a perfect world this could be a possibility, but we do not live in a perfect world. If everyone is safe, but your organization fails to perform, it fails. If everyone is safe, but the market dries up, you fail.

Let's put on our semantic simplification cap and say what we really mean. Is safety important? Yes! Lack of safety could lead to death, environmental damage, reputational issues, financial loss, organizational failure, economic hardship, and much more. Is safety really first? No way! There are many other factors critical for success. So, what is safety?

"Safety is Critical"

That's what it is, and that's the truth! By saying, "Safety is Critical," you are not a liar, don't enable dependence on others and stress the seriousness of the subject in a way everyone can relate to.

Simply changing context to many of the overcomplicated terms we use today so their meanings are easier for everyone to understand will go a long way to preventing the concrete barrier disconnects caused by unclear expectations.

For evidence of the destruction caused to organizations by unclear expectations, all you have to do is look around.

1. Does your organization have an information purgatory where expectations exist but are rarely read?

2. Is there a room, you know the one I'm talking about, where there are shelves upon shelves of operating procedures and manuals that have sat untouched for so long their dust has started gathering dust?

3. Do you attend meetings where critical information is shared with you and never disseminated down to the front-line workers?

4. Do important emails get lost in your inbox because you get too many or don't have time?

5. Do you sometimes complete tasks without following the instructions, or figure out how to do something on your own due to lack of guidance or instructions?

These may seem like ridiculous questions to ask because you probably answered yes to most, if not all, of them. That's exactly why they are so scary.

> We are caught in a whirlpool of destruction that is rapidly becoming stronger than we can escape from.

The taboo is becoming the norm, selfishness is trumping ethics, and the unacceptable is becoming expected. To save ourselves from drowning in the whirlpool to destruction, we must acknowledge we are trapped in it, stop thinking we are strong enough to swim out of it alone, and start seeking better paths to success.

Eradication Methods

For an organization to avoid creating unclear expectations, they must first understand what success means to them and then articulate how they are going to get there.

Many organizations attempt to articulate their expectations for success, only to fall short when they don't thoroughly understand what pitfalls to avoid or how to respond to unwanted events.

Usually, an organization either hires a 3rd party who doesn't understand their culture to develop their expectations for them or throws a bunch of their employees in a room to battle it out. Both of these approaches have their perks--I mean who doesn't love a good fight--but also come with hefty costs because they don't take the organization's risks or culture into account.

Reducing risks and simplification are the best methods organizations can use to clearly understand and articulate success.

Risk Reduction

We tend to view organizational risks in financial terms, when risk actually lies in everything we do.

Organizations use different terminology to break out their risk categories, so I've generalized risks into the three categories of performance, people and public for the purposes of this series, which are described below:

Risk Categories (Three P's)

- **Performance** – includes financial, operating, asset, and quality related risks, etc.

- **People** – includes employee retention, culture, health and safety, diversity, etc.

- **Public** – Includes customer satisfaction, market demands, reputations, stakeholders, community outreach, environmental responsibility, etc.

Failure to understand your organization's risks is a recipe for disaster! The secret is to identify and understand all possible risks to your organization. Doing so will enable you to establish controls to prevent unwanted events from occurring and put mitigations in place to lessen the severity of loss after unwanted events occur.

For an organization to have a strong foundation it must have a comprehensive risk management process defined in its OPALS. Many organizations have a risk management process; however, very few are all-inclusive, having multiple different processes for different types of risks.

Every risk-management process should incorporate the five of risk-reduction (A5rr) shown below to help clearly define and support sustainable success (Image 5).

Image 5 - A5rr Diagram

A5rr Elements

1. Acknowledge

- Identify All Risks (Register)
- Recognize Emerging Risks

2. Assess

- Assess risks/emerging risks
- Assess Barrier Performance
- Review Other Inputs (Learn)

3. Act

- Prioritize Risk Plans/Actions
- Leadership Endorsements
- Communicate Risks and Plan
- Update Related Documents

4. Assure

- Confirm Barrier Strength
- Monitor Performance

5. Adjust

- Track Actions to Closure
- Review & Update Regularly
- Apply Learnings

The Bowtie Method

Most organizations, especially in regulation-rich Countries like the United States, rely on the government to define their risks for them. These types of organizations tend to base most of their expectations on regulations and laws, with risk departments primarily focused on financial risks only.

This compliance-based approach is a lot like going to the hardware store to buy a good quality hammer but purchasing a toolbox full of cheap tools you don't need because it's on sale.

Laws and regulations only exist for known issues and are usually written to apply to a large audience. They are not specific to your organization's needs, and tend to cause confusion, hinder performance and in some cases introduce risks.

In the parts of the world where the governments have not developed extensive laws and regulations, many organizations apply a risk-based approach when defining their expectations.

In my opinion, the United States should follow this trend and eliminate a majority of the regulatory burden suffocating organizations and their ability to survive and thrive in our ever-growing competitive world. With that said, I do see the value in the information contained in the existing regulations but believe they would be better suited as guidance documents available for organizations to review when assessing their risks.

There are numerous methods to assess risks, each with different strengths. I've found the easiest and most effective method to use when developing expectations is the Bowtie methodology, which is illustrated in Image 6.

If you are in an industry familiar with this methodology, you are ahead of the game! The Bowtie method gained popularity amongst oil and gas organizations in the early 1990's after the 1988 Piper Alpha incident. Since then, it is most commonly used to assess catastrophic, safety-related risks.

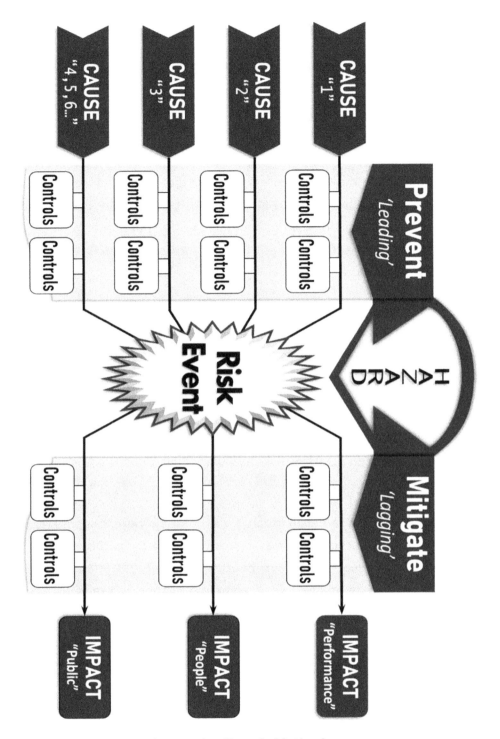

Image 6 - Bowtie Method

The Bowtie is a great tool for assessing process related-risks but can become quite complicated when the engineers start diving into the details of every valve, pipe and process.

I was introduced to the Bowtie method while working in the alternative energy section for a large oil and gas organization. Leadership informed me that we were required to rate our risks on their standardized risk matrix and then use the Bowtie method to assess any risks that scored high enough on our risk matrix. Since I was not familiar with Bowties way back then, I immediately sought out opportunities to get up to speed quickly, reading literature, watching videos and attending the organization's training program for Bowtie facilitators.

Initially, I was skeptical. At the time I was much younger and was already respected in my field as a builder and fixer of management systems. What were they going to tell me that I didn't already know? What made this method different than the countless others I had been using successfully to this point? I didn't know it then, but my world was about to be rocked!

Upon being introduced to the tool, lightbulbs in my brain began turning on. For so long, I had been assessing risks based on regulations, missing so many pieces of the puzzle.

Have you ever utilized James Reason's Swiss cheese model to assess risks? (https://en.wikipedia.org/wiki/Swiss_cheese_model) Even though it is a respected tool, its scope is limited because it only looks at the barriers between the hazard and the event, completely ignoring the mitigations needed to lessen the severity of impacts after the event occurs.

The Bowtie method, however, looks at both sides of the event and is extremely easy to use. It's so easy to use that I apply it in my personal life as much, if not more, than I do at work. As long as you keep things simple, it will be a great tool to use when building your organization's path to success.

The Bowtie method
will help your organization

1. Identify and assess risks

2. Define clear expectations that align leadership and the workforce with its vision of success.

3. Highlight specific leading indicators that can be reported, tracked and measured on your path to success.

4. Communicate more effectively, preventing concrete barrier disconnects caused by unclear expectations.

5. Foster cultures of understanding, loyalty and trust.

Books, websites, software and training are available if you would like to learn more about Bowties. In addition, I will be covering the importance of taking a risk-based approach and more on the Bowtie methodology later in the Deadly Practices series.

Once you understand your risks better, then simplification becomes, well a whole lot simpler!

Simplification

Albert Einstein once advocated for keeping things as simple as possible, but not simpler. I agree. After all, who am I to question Einstein?

In the Merriam-Webster dictionary, simple is defined as "readily understood or performed". The goal of simplification is to improve efficiency, effectiveness, performance and quality with the least amount of effort.

It's practically impossible to simplify anything when more than one person is tug-of-warring over priorities. Now, multiply that by tens, hundreds or even thousands to see what a mess is created when organizations allow everyone to put in their two cents. For proof, simply read a legal document!

Therefore, if senior leadership overcomplicates their expectations at the foundational level, it will just get worse as they trickle through the concrete ceiling.

This is why it is so important to simplify wherever possible, and the best place to start is at the very top.

Organizations who develop their OPALS, clearly define success, and take a risk-based approach when defining their expectations are well positioned to keep things simple.

The following are some easy to remember simplification tips that you'll want to consider every time expectations are developed and modified.

Simplification Tips

1. Chop Chop

Say everything, half it, and then half it again.

2. Elementary

Say it so a third-grader can understand.

3. Keep it Real

Say only what you expect others to deliver.

4. Use it or Lose it

Say it only if you will walk the talk.

5. Semantics

Say what you mean.

6. Standardize

Say it really well once.

Now that you understand the importance of having clearly defined expectations, take a few minutes to review the next steps, reflect on what your organization needs, and write down your commitments to impact positive changes on the blank Reflections and Commitments pages in the back of the book.

Next Steps

1. Ensure your risk management process incorporates performance, people and public factors when assessing risks and decisions.

2. Utilize a risk-based approach to help better understand the risks your organization faces and the controls and mitigations necessary to support sustainable success.

3. Conduct review sessions to identify vague and overcomplicated expectations, simplifying verbiage and eliminating waste throughout your entire organization.

4. Where unclear expectations are identified, develop a plan to simplify terminology, and eliminate confusion throughout your organization.

5. When in doubt, reach out for help. Schedule a consultation with a qualified OPALS Executive Coach for assistance evaluating the clarity of your expectations, conducting culture assessments to gauge understanding, updating your risk assessment process and facilitating Bowties.

DP 3

Unbalanced Expectations

"The first responsibility of a leader is to define reality. The last is to say thank you. In between, the leader is a servant."

Max De Pree

We have already established the importance of defining your expectations and making sure they clearly express what is needed for your organization to succeed, but we still need to discuss the consequences that result when an organization's expectations are unbalanced.

For years I've been attempting to educate leaders around the world about this Deadly Practice but have yet to see many organizations do this well. Plenty attempt to find balance but fall short when leadership makes decisions without considering the possible impacts thoroughly.

Most decisions are made with good intentions. Unfortunately, even the best intentions can backfire when too much focus is put in one area, causing risks to increase in other areas. This is one reason I sometimes refer to "Focus" as "Fuckus". Time and time again I've seen organizations fail because their well-intentioned decisions end up consuming valuable resources needed by others.

Integrating in the recommendations from the previous section will help you develop a well-balanced organization. If your expectations are defined and clear, they will make it through the concrete barrier. Unfortunately, unbalanced expectations can derail your efforts, preventing your organization from successfully traversing the path to success and attaining the culture of success necessary to survive and thrive (Image 7).

It is extremely important to make sure our expectations are balanced and remain balanced. Don't get me wrong, change is going to continue happening. What we need to improve is how to impact positive change.

We are all humans, and humans are amazing creatures capable of independent thought, emotions and feelings. In addition to these wonderful traits, we also have needs, desires, demands and behaviors that do not always align with what is best for the organization. This rings true for the owner of the organization all of the way down to the contractor who vacuums the floors.

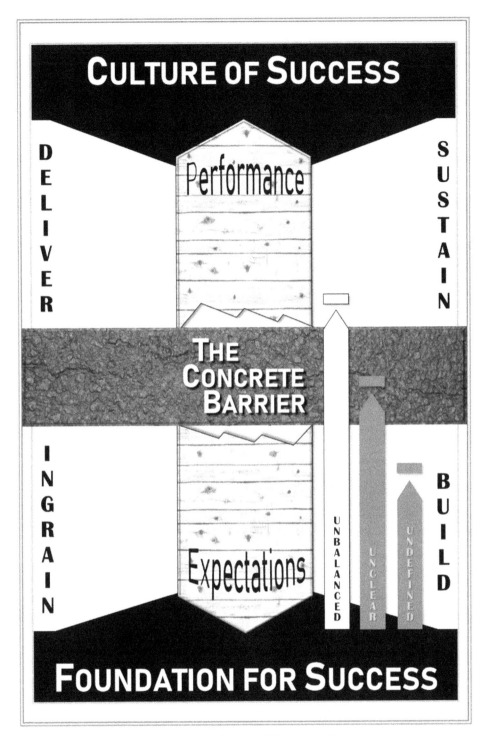

Image 7 – Unbalanced Expectations

63

Leaders need to be able to recognize this Deadly Practice when it strikes. Notice I said

"when" it strikes, and not
"if" it strikes.

The biggest challenge with this Deadly Practice is that there are so many factors that can throw an organization off balance. Yet senior leadership rarely recognizes how unbalanced things are until it's too late. One of the reasons for this is because leaders are becoming less in-tune with their workforce. Data overload, excessive meetings and cost-cutting efforts make it difficult for leaders to spend quality time with their employees.

Unfortunately, when an organization's expectations are unbalanced, the workforce begins to question leadership's motives, enabling a culture of distrust to form.

Culture of Distrust

Lack of trust throughout your workforce acts like a cancer, spreading silently and striking quickly. Also, like cancer, it can be extremely difficult to eradicate once it sinks its fangs in. A culture of distrust can kill an organization's ability to succeed quickly or slowly over time. This is why it is so important to address unbalanced expectations immediately.

There are a thousand examples I can give to support the devastating impacts a culture of distrust can cause. You probably already have a few popping into your head right now!

Unbalanced expectations usually lie at the heart of trust issues because whenever one thing is viewed as more important than another, those on the less-important end of the stick are left wondering why. Below are just a few examples of how "good intentions" turn into viscous success snipers.

Unbalanced
Incentive Programs

All you have to do is observe how our destructive, current, so-called incentive programs backfire to understand what I mean here. I've gone through just about every different type of incentive program there is, and there are so many Deadly Practices caused by them that I will be dedicating multiple books in the series to the topic. For now, I'll just give you the big picture to add perspective.

Whenever an organization incentivizes its workforce on lagging indicators, which are the indicators that result after something has already happened, not only does it set itself up for failure by being behind the ball from the get-go, but it also fosters distrust. Why? Because lagging indicators usually look at results of efforts related to multiple different factors. Being scrutinized for an end result you don't have complete control over can easily lead to pointing anger, resentment, blame and the desire to take matters into your own hands.

For example, if mid-level leaders are incentivized to reach a set revenue or profit target every month to receive their bonus, they will do everything they can to reach that goal. Heck, they have bills to pay and egos to protect. Unfortunately, revenue and profit results are lagging indicators attained through a compilation of many different people's decisions and efforts that they cannot directly control. They cannot control senior leadership's decisions any more than they can control the market. All they can control is the culture and performance they are responsible for. Unfortunately, having a weak foundation limits their ability to even do that well, as discussed previously.

Also, let's not forget the loaded weapon we give this "good intention" when we limit our employee's potential for earning their full incentive with the much-hated bell curve, and throw in favoritism and unclear expectations for measuring success.

Wow! Can you spell

D-O-O-M-E-D?

What we need to do is STOP what we're doing and shift 180 degrees towards a more balanced approach. I've seen a few industries try but fall short when they only address part of the problem.

The following illustrates the difference between the method most commonly used now and what a better approach might look like.

Annual Goals	Results	Bonus	Fair
1) Increase revenue by 5%	A. 7% B. 3%	A. Yes B. No	?
2) Zero lost time accidents	A. 0 B. 2	A. Yes B. No	?
3) Customer satisfaction >95%	A. 97% B. 85%	A. Yes B. No	?
4) Employee satisfaction >90%	A. 98% B. 75%	A. Yes B. No	?

Table 1 - Unbalanced Approach

Table 1 represents an organization that bases its incentives on lagging indicators. For the purposes of our discussion, A and B represent two plant managers that work for the same organization whose plants are located in adjacent lots from each other but produce different products.

66

The reason question marks are in the earned column is because even though the plant managers might have some control over how well their site performs, there are many other factors that impact lagging indicators.

For example, what if the organization's senior leadership cut budgets halfway through the year that impact one more than the other, rolls out a massive advertising campaign for widget A and not widget B, or conducts multiple audits of site B that hinder the site's ability to perform or harms morale? Also, basing bonuses in incidents is a slippery slope. Sure, the plant manager can foster a strong safety culture, but can they really prevent all unwanted events from occurring? What if the cause of the incident is related to an employee exposure from years ago, or happened off-the-job and the employee created an incident to receive time off and compensation from the organization?

Designing incentives based on lagging indicators can easily backfire as well. What if manager B noticed their numbers were not going to be enough to get their bonus? Could they be negatively incentivized to deter reporting, inflate revenue projections, bribe customers and bully their workforce into filling out positive employee surveys? They definitely could!

Sadly, these unethical behaviors are extremely common. If you think otherwise, just look at the chaos left behind when a great manager decides to leave an organization, and everyone left must clean up the mess they secretly made.

Yes, there are dozens of other reasons leaders act unethically, which we'll be covering in more detail throughout the series. However, if you are brave enough to find out why they were able to get away with it, you'll often learn that foundational weaknesses not only allowed their poor behaviors, but also encouraged it by not being defined, clear and balanced.

Table 2 illustrates what an incentive plan based on leading indicators might include.

Annual Goals	Results	Bonus	Fair
1) Develop, implement and track your resourcing and operating plan in alignment with your budget.	A. Thorough B. Incomplete	A. Yes B. No	YES
2) Participate in 20% of risk assessments.	A. Complete B. Incomplete	A. Yes B. No	YES
3) Conduct and document weekly observations and learnings sessions with the workforce.	A. Complete B. Incomplete	A. Yes B. No	YES
4) Conduct quarterly alignment gap assessments and culture surveys.	A. Thorough B. Incomplete	A. Yes B. No	YES

Table 2 - Balanced Approach

The plant managers are in complete control of ensuring these goals get completed, and assuming they align with the organization's expectations for success, should help create the desired culture and performance for success.

The absence of numerical scores in the Results column is purposeful and extremely important. As soon as a lagging indicator is tied to a goal, it poses an immediate risk of becoming unbalanced and ineffective.

As I alluded to earlier, incentives also become drastically unbalanced when an organization utilizes the bell curve and permits subjectiveness in the rating process. Mind you, this is much harder to accomplish when the goals are based on measurable leading indicators, but still can occur if a rating scale is used without agreement from leadership and the employee. I've been on the delivering and receiving end of good and bad rating processes and can vouch for the damage done to trust when the goals are exceeded, only for the employee to get a "meets expectation" rating because their leader can only award a set number of employees the prestigious "exceeds expectations" badge of honor.

Why can't everyone exceed expectations?

If you have ever worked for an organization and been told that "exceeds expectations" are rarely awarded, and only if you reinvent the wheel, then I am confident you have worked where a culture of distrust existed as a result of unbalanced expectations. Anyone who disagrees needs to buy a huge mirror and stare into it until they have the courage to remove the wool blindfold and face reality.

Not only do goals need to be fair and based on leading indicators that are within the individual's span of control, but success needs to be attainable too. How in the heck can an organization expect to attain success and grow sustainably if they tell 68 percent of their workforce, they are average? I can't think of anything else more demeaning and damaging than expecting your employees to deliver gold and paying them with big stinking bags of crap. Can you?

Let's not leave out how costly an unbalanced incentive program is for an organization. Every year organizations shell out billions of dollars to incentivize success, and what do they get for it? Underperformance, unethical behavior and untrusting employees, that's what!

If you are nodding your head in agreement but throwing your arms up in frustration while doubting the existence of a solution to this problem, then you are not alone. I've been in your shoes time and time again. It wasn't until I thoroughly understood the risks and applied the Bowtie method to this problem that the solutions became much clearer. Building a balanced incentive process is possible for those brave enough to try something different. Before reviewing methods to accomplish this nirvana, it's important to understand how the decisions we make at work and in our personal lives can, and often sadly do, lead to the failure of the clearest, most balanced programs.

Unthoughtful Decisions

Have you ever worked for an organization that made changes more often than you changed your socks? If yes, welcome to the club! If no, where do you work, and are they hiring?

Change is often necessary and can be great. But far too often it does more harm than good. Especially when changes are made without thought of balance and consequences.

Like the Deadly Practices we've discussed already, I could give you hundreds of examples where change has created new problems, made things worse or led to destruction. You can probably list off a dozen or more right now as well. Below are just a few destructive changes that happen frequently around the globe:

1. New leadership lacks competency for the role.
2. New leader's values do not align with the organization's values.
3. Quick-fix solutions to one problem cause one or more problems elsewhere.
4. New and updated requirements are implemented without defined delivery expectations or trained personnel to maximize the value of the tool.
5. Equipment installed without consideration for process flow or operator safety.
6. Budget cuts and workforce reductions made without considering impacts to quality or future performance.

7. Mergers and acquisitions completed without consolidation of processes, education of personnel or alignment of cultures.

8. Action items assigned after events (e.g.: audits, incidents, etc.) without consideration for resource limitations.

Whenever decisions are made without considering the balance between performance, people and the public, we often end up fuckusing too much in one area which increases risks in other areas.

Sadly, when this occurs, the ones who tend to take the blame for poor performance are the ones impacted by the increased risks from someone else's unbalanced decisions. An example of this would be when senior leadership decides to lay off employees when the market shifts (e.g.: recent oil and gas market drop) without considering the number, experience or skills of personnel physically needed to deliver sustainable success.

I've been told that many organizations take this opportunity to clean out the poor performers. Unfortunately, that's rarely the case. Instead, the more senior and experienced employees leave first, often taking retirement packages to buy out their loyalty to the organization. Then, those with stronger skillsets and higher salaries go next. Finally, it comes down to who likes who best, which often favors the yes-folks and sends the innovative go getters straight to the unemployment line.

Let's fast forward a bit. The organization is now demanding more of less employees and morale is low because of anger and fear. Those who were laid off have found other jobs, possibly with competitors. Expectations are being performed when possible, and usually to minimum standards at best. Errors increase because knowledge and know-how are gone. Quality is poor, performance is down, etc.

So, who gets blamed when a customer calls demanding a full refund because they are unhappy with the quality or the plant blows up because the equipment wasn't properly maintained? Is it the senior leadership who demanded layoffs, or is it the quality inspector, maintenance manager or plant manager who take the fall?

Some organizations have great root cause investigation processes and will eventually identify where the issues began, but usually fingers point to those trying to survive the unbalanced decisions of others.

Another example of the destruction done by unbalanced decisions is the November 8, 2018 wildfire that swept through the town of Paradise and surrounding areas, destroying nearly 14,000 homes and killing at least 88 people. There are many insinuations about the reasons for the devastation the wildfire caused. According to various news sources, the combination of heat, drought and high winds enabled the fire to cause so much damage. Many are pointing fingers at climate change.

My opinion, after living and working in California, is that California is hot, dry, windy in areas and prone to wildfires. That's what it is, and probably will be for a long time. So, what good does it do to keep blaming climate change and mother nature for death and destruction? Absolutely none!

What we need to do is step back and look at unbalanced decisions that have been made that allow mother nature to wreak so much havoc. By considering the three P's, we might ask:

1. **Performance:** Have the California firefighters been conducting controlled burns in areas where wildfire risks are highest? What other preventative efforts are being taken to prevent wildfires? Were homes built to lessen the impacts of wildfires? Do insurance companies provide regular fire safety assessments and offer preventative planning guidance?

2. **People:** Are people who live in areas at risk for wildfires educated on methods to prevent, prepare for and respond to wildfires? Are people held accountable for taking preventative measures?

3. Public: Are environmental protected species regulations preventing homeowners and municipalities from removing dried plant matter? Are regulations adequately controlling air emissions from nearby industrial organizations to reduce flammable chemicals in the air?

By considering the three P's when making decisions, organizations will prevent introducing unnecessary risks and maximize the return on their investments.

Eradication Methods

Have you heard the saying, "Nothing's fair in love and war"? Well, this is business, so let's leave the hugging and fighting out of it and create a balanced and fair organization where your employees will want to come to work every day and you'll reap the rewards from taking the path to success.

Creating balance is not easy or something you can do once and forget about. Maintaining balance is a full-time effort, 24 hours a day, seven days a week, 365.2422 days a year! This may sound daunting, and possibly even impossible, but let me reassure you that it can be accomplished if you have the right processes in place and competent leaders to support your organization. Without those elements your organization might as well be walking on a tightrope over Manhattan without a safety net, at risk of falling to a dismal fate when the wind starts blowing. And trust me, it will start blowing!

The following are the most critical eradication methods every organization should incorporate when building their foundation for success.

Balanced Decisions

I've been speaking about the importance of balance around the world for years, and the hardest part has been clearly demonstrating the impacts created by our decisions. Using a two-tray balancing scale won't work because there needs to be at least three trays to account for all three P's.

After much research, it became clear that the tool we needed didn't exist. Instead of trying to make a square peg fit into a round hole, I decided to build a round peg, and developed the Decision/Impact Scale. This tool, shown in Image 8, stimulates balanced and thoughtful discussions when making decisions. Here's the best part!

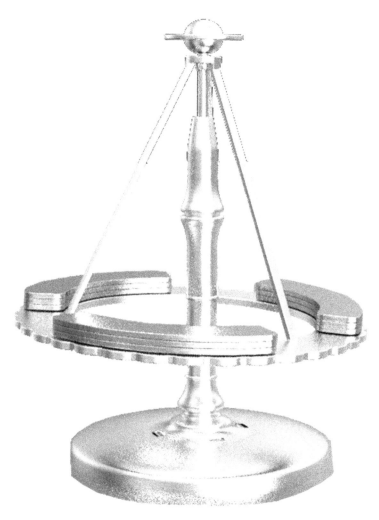

Image 8 – Decision/Impact Scale

There is no right or wrong, too much or too little. The value comes from considering the potential impacts of your decisions, identifying opportunities to maintain balance and making changes that propel you towards a Culture of Success.

In Chapter 3, we discussed utilizing the Bowtie method to assess risks for a better understanding of what is needed versus not. If you want to add more value to your discussions, the controls and mitigations from bowties can be referenced when using the Decision/Impact Scale.

The Decision/Impact Scale is a circular balance with three spaces, one for each of the three P's, to stack weights onto. The goal is to find balance when considering the risks related to any decision. Simply stack the weights onto the space that correlates with the controls and mitigations that will be in place related to the decision you are pondering. If the scale is not balanced, you will be able to clearly see where there is too much focus and where risks may be increased if additional considerations are not taken into account (Image 9).

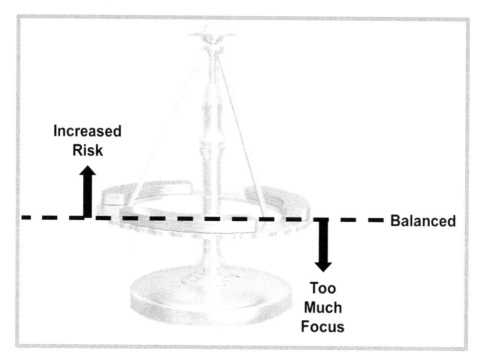

Image 9 - Decision/Impact Scale Function

The scale is intended to be used as a tool to spark healthy discussions when contemplating decisions. You will be amazed how much the quality of your discussions will increase and the value that will be gained by pulling everyone's noses away from the slideshow and their phones, and physically engaging their minds in the decision-balancing process!

In the future I would like to develop an online interactive Artificial Intelligence Decision/Impact assessment tool for organizations to use. Until then, I hope you will consider utilizing the scale, or at least its concept, the next time you contemplate a decision.

It's that simple!

Standardization

Standardization is a framework of agreements to which all relevant parties in an organization align with to ensure consistent delivery of the expectations necessary for achieving sustainable success.

Standardization is achieved by setting generally accepted expectations regarding how a business is operated or how certain required processes are governed. The goal of standardization is to eliminate redundancies and decrease the opportunity for errors.

One of the most objective ways to simplify organizational processes is to standardize recurring and identical processes.

"If managed properly, standardized work establishes a relationship between people and their work processes. This relationship can enhance ownership and pride in the quality of work performance. The result is high morale and productivity," according to Walter W. McIntyre, in his book, "Lean and Mean Process Improvement".

Unfortunately, like simplification, our egos and selfishness tend to prevent us from standardizing with the intent of the organization's success in mind. Instead, leaders kick and claw to maintain their independence, and then complain when they don't have enough time to keep up with everything. It's extremely unfortunate and a complete waste of resources.

This is an area where organizations need to hold the line. By giving in to the demands of the masses, organizations unintentionally shoot themselves in the foot. Where duplication of efforts exists, there is waste. Where waste exists, there is opportunity.

Do not confuse standardization with lack of innovation. By eliminating inefficiencies, confusion and conflict, employees will stop having to waste time and gain the time and energy to focus on innovation and growth.

The best way to start is from the top with the organization's OPALS and then work your way down through the organization wherever top-level standardization is not possible.

Consider the following when standardizing your expectations for success:

1. Begin by defining the governance and nomenclature to be used consistently across the organization. Speaking the same language and knowing who to go to for what will improve buy-in and loyalty both ways.

2. Build in room for flexibility and individuality by utilizing templates with fields that can be modified, and a process for deviations. This creates the feeling of independence and ownership without increasing risk for the organization.

3. Automate processes wherever possible, improving consistency while providing employees with valuable time to work on more important initiatives.

4. Utilize information management solutions to capture and report important information.

5. Don't be bullied by advisory staff. Ask a legal, risk management, human resources and safety person to work together on one initiative and end up with four conflicting opinions on how to get it done. Remember, leadership owns responsibility for the organization, while everyone else is there in an advisory role. Ultimately, what matters is what's needed to result in sustainable success, and how to accomplish it. Base your decisions off your risk assessments and risk comfort level, then be prepared to respond if things don't go perfectly according to plan.

Balanced Incentive Process

Hindering people's ability to exceed our expectations, and on the flip side, giving everyone a prize for merely breathing, fosters resentment, distrust and complacency. This is the opposite of the intent of incentives and a huge waste of valuable resources.

What we need to do is START incentivizing individuals, both positively and constructively, for their achievements based on leading indicators using measurable goals that do not leave room for bias.

The best way to eradicate this problem is to balance your incentive process, considering the eradication methods recommended in the previous chapters. The condensed steps are listed for you below:

1. Clearly define success for the organization.

2. Develop expectations that clearly show the workforce what they are accountable for delivering and how it aligns with your organization's definition of success.

3. Define and deliver incentives, both positive and constructive, based on performance.

4. Create organization-wide goals that align with your mission, vision, values and expectations.

5. Utilize the controls identified by the Bowtie method to build individualized and measurable goals that are necessary for successful performance.

6. Base the incentives on measurable factors to eliminate bias.

7. Use a clear measurement structure for rating performance, where feedback between leadership and the employee is reviewed and a mutually agreed upon rating is determined. Then, tabulate and

average all of the ratings to calculate an objective and fair performance score.

8.   Ensure your leadership is competent to implement the process consistently.

9.   Educate the workforce on the balanced approach.

10. Create paths for issues and questions to be voiced, evaluated and responded to in a timely manner.

11. Take steps to assure the process is followed.

12. Hold everyone accountable for conformance.

13. Survey the workforce and assess the process regularly to identify learnings and continuous improvement opportunities.

<u>Management of Change (MoC)</u>

The last eradication method I'd like to share with you will actually be covered in Book 4 of the Deadly Expectations set. I am including the highlights of it here because it is extremely important to define a process for managing change when building your foundation of success. I cannot stress this enough.

Ironically, in the United States, MoC is a regulatory requirement defined in the Process Safety Management of Highly Hazardous Chemicals standard (29 CFR 1910.119) that ONLY applies to areas that meet the definition of a covered process.

What's the big deal? As long as we have controls in place to address the process risks, which have the potential to cause catastrophe in epic proportions, who cares about the other stuff? Wouldn't MoC just overcomplicate things, slow down performance and waste valuable resources?

Sadly, this type of thinking, in addition to the "I don't have to, so I'm not going to" mentality is what leads organizations down the expressway to destruction. So many leaders boast about their commitment to workplace safety and level of compliance when they integrate MoC processes in regulated areas. Unfortunately, failing to apply a comprehensive MoC process consistently across the entire organization, regardless of regulations, adds unnecessary complexity that leads to confusion and results in errors – all while wasting valuable resources. Sounds a lot like Success Suicide to me!

This serves as a great example of where organizations should build their OPALS based on risks and not regulations.

A strong Management of Change process will be standardized across the entire organization, and encompass asset, administrative and personnel changes. Examples of the types of changes that should trigger the MoC process are listed in Table 3.

Asset	Administrative	Personnel
- Equipment	- Policies	- Leadership
- Processes	- Procedures	- Machine operators
- Buildings	- Guidelines	- Technical authorities
- Materials	- Training materials	- Other critical roles

Table 3 - MoC Triggers

When built well, a Management of Change process will help organizations prepare for change and maintain balance when implementing their decisions. The result? A knowledgeable workforce aligned towards integrating balanced and beneficial changes necessary for success.

Next Steps

1. There are no quick fixes for maintaining balance in your organization. Doing so requires ongoing efforts and resources.

   ✓ Include processes in your OPALS that support sustainable growth and success while lessening the burden of this ongoing balancing act.

   ✓ Utilize the Decision/Impact Scale to spark conversations and considerations when pondering decisions at work, in public and at home. If you are interested in using this tool in meetings or would like to provide one to all of your employees, various versions are available for purchase online.

2. Wherever possible, standardize! The goal is to standardize the who, what, when, where, why and how necessary to deliver sustainable success. For this to work, organizations need to leave independent agendas and egos in the parking lot, and ensure strategic flexibility is baked into all expectations to allow for differences without jeopardizing their intent.

Next Steps (Continued)

3. Ensure your incentive process is fostering a healthy workplace culture and delivering the ROI intended by building a fair, proactive and objective approach. Utilize measurable goals based on leading indicators that are within the worker's span of control, encourage excellence by using an objective review process and hold individuals accountable for their performance.

4. Incorporate a Management of Change process into your OPALS to help ensure the potential impacts to your organization's balance are considered when making decisions across the entire organization. The intent of this process is to solicit discussions around risks related to a specific decisions/change, identify the risk reduction measures necessary to maintain balance and to authorize and verify that those measures are executed to support sustainable success.

Conclusion

"We cannot solve our problems
with the same thinking we used
when we created them."

Albert Einstein

This first book lays the groundwork for the entire series. An organization must build a strong enough foundation to support its growth, withstand changes and deliver sustainable success.

To build a strong foundation, an organization must ensure that it defines what success is and develops clear and balanced expectations necessary to guide their organization along the path to success towards a sustainable Culture of Success (Image 10).

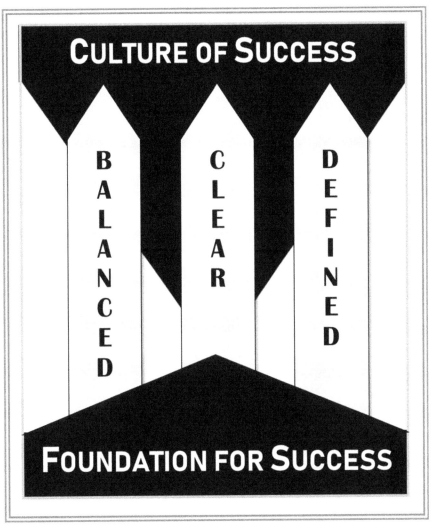

Image 10 - A Foundation Built for Success

To recap, the three most common Deadly Practices that occur when building an organization's foundation for success are:

1.   Undefined Expectations ➔ Culture of Ignorance

2.   Unclear Expectations ➔ Culture of Confusion

3.   Unbalanced Expectations ➔ Culture of Distrust

Failure to eradicate these Deadly Practices may not lead to your organization's immediate destruction but will continue to cause cracks in your foundation and irreversible damage to your culture until something gives. It's only a matter of time.

Your first priorities should be on building and strengthening your foundation of success by assessing your existing systems and eradicating Deadly Expectations.

Stay vigilant, and never forget that "best practices" do not exist, "safety is not first", less is more, and it's okay to make mistakes as long as you learn something and improve from them.

Take a moment to review the following Reflection Questions and jot down your responses on the reflection and commitments section in the back of the book.

Book 1
Reflection Questions

1. How could clearly defining your personal and organizational mission, vision, values and expectations, gain you more space?

2. How could admitting your current organization is vulnerable to Deadly Practices make you more powerful?

3. How might honesty and transparency make you more respected throughout your organization?

4. How could simplifying and standardizing your expectations using an approach aimed at reducing risks instead of compliance make you more connected with the workforce?

5. How might measuring leading indicators and celebrating failures result in better outcomes?

The Journey Forward

"Success is not final; failure is not fatal: It is the courage to continue that counts."

Winston S. Churchill

So, what's next? Where do we go from here? The truth is, we still have such a long way to go. If only I had the ability to lie and tell you that defining clear and balanced expectations will solve all of your problems, but I cannot. I also don't have a magic bean or quick fix solution. Heck, those are the types of things that got us into the mess we're in now; so, with hope, experience has taught you to run the other way if anyone says they do.

This book barely scratches the surface of the changes we need to make if we want the world to be a better place in the future and this series is merely one of many stepping stones along my journey.

T.A. Laser's Commitment

I dream of a future where my children and their children's children travel the paths to success built by those before them. My personal commitment is to continue sharing as much as I can for as long as I'm able. The following are a few of the ways I plan on delivering on my commitment.

Organization Culture Killers

As mentioned previously, this is the first book of many in the Organization Culture Killers, Deadly Practices series. With so many more learnings and tools to share, the books are practically writing themselves! I would love to hear from you if you'd like to share your learnings, or if you're interested in collaborating on future books.

Speaking and Coaching

I have been educating, motivating and mentoring leaders and professionals throughout my career and plan to continue doing so. Books are great tools to reach a wide audience; however, I've found the best way to inspire and motivate others is when multiple senses are engaged. My energetic keynotes and workshops combine emotion, interaction, honesty and valuable information professionals need to build better paths to success. I would love the opportunity to deliver a keynote or workshop for your students, organization or community. If interested in learning more, or if you would like me to speak at your next event, visit www.talaser.com/speaker.

Gap and Culture Assessments

I will be working with organizations who want to improve on and eliminate Deadly Practices. The best way I've found to do this is through gap assessments and culture assessments. I'm talking about hands-on, in-depth assessments with all people throughout the organizational chain. Working this way allows me to see the actual gaps and coach executives on making more thoughtful changes for a more sustainable succession in the future.

Learning and Continuous Improvement Workgroups

Big-thinking visionaries motivate me. The best way to facilitate huge change and innovation is to gather the brightest minds and unite them in a common cause. This is exactly what Herbert Hoover did as the Secretary of Commerce in the 1920's during the creation and construction of the Hoover Dam. He commissioned brilliant engineers, economists, businessmen and government officials to come up with solutions to create jobs and construct an incredible project that converted water from the Colorado River into hydroelectric power for the Southwestern United States. To help businesses, organizations, and agencies simplify, standardize and increase efficiency and purpose, I am planning to coordinate workgroups around the world in the near future.

Education and Textbook Adaptation

The sooner we can expose young people and future leaders to these proven concepts, the better. My plan is to condense this series into a textbook format, and then provide high school teachers and collegiate professors with the information and tools necessary to transfer the knowledge to the next generations of executives, influencers and leaders.

Children's Books

Why wait until high school or college? At an early age we begin learning how to manage things, follow the rules and pass the test. Our education systems are not very good at teaching us the leadership skills we will need to be successful, and with parents pulling in the reins of control tighter and tighter, children aren't getting the valuable leadership skills learned from the life of Hard Knocks either. The sooner we can teach our children about leadership, strong foundations and pitfalls to avoid, the better This is why I am planning to translate, with the help of educators and children, each Organizational Culture Killers book in the series into children's books as well.

Your Path to Success

Congratulations! Beginning the Journey towards impacting positive change can be scary, which is why I am so glad you have demonstrated the curiosity and courage to take the leap and ride the wave!

I'd love to say the Journey gets easier from here, but that isn't the case. We have a long way to go if we want to repair the destruction Deadly Practices have already wrought. The Journey will be challenging, requiring support from you and others in epic proportions, but with time and perseverance, we can begin laying the groundwork essential for building better paths to success.

How are you feeling? Are you excited to jump in and start impacting change, or are you overwhelmed with the enormity of it all?

Trying to tackle everything at once is like eating an elephant whole. It's painful and extremely unhealthy.

Your toolbox has some great tools in it now! The question is, what are you going to do with them?

Hiding them in the corner of your garage won't make the problems go away.

Using them incorrectly could make things worse.

Your time is valuable, and it's important you get a return on your investment. The only way for this to be possible is if you physically do something with the nuggets of value you uncovered along the Journey.

1. Revisit the reflections and commitments you've been jotting down along our Journey through the Deadly Expectations forest riddled with Deadly Practices..

2. Prioritize the changes that have the potential to positively impact your organization the most.

3. Develop realistic action items.

4. Take the steps necessary to get'er done!

5. Share what you've learned with others and INSPIRE FORWARD!

6. Once the wheels are in motion, continue reading the books in the Deadly Practices Series. Each book builds upon the previous, providing you with clear, simple-to-follow, blueprints for building a Culture of Success. Book 2 reveals the Deadly Practices created when leadership attempts to ingrain expectations that are unknown, unaccepted and unsupported.

Now that you have the tools, what are you going to build first?

Acknowledgments

This book series is a culmination of my experiences and learnings, input from thousands of other individuals and knowledge gathered from hundreds of books over nearly five decades. Listing everyone who has inspired, mentored and supported me would take its own book. I am extremely grateful that so many amazing people have crossed my path throughout life and would like to thank a few of those who helped guide me along my own personal path to sustainable success.

First, I would like to thank my children and husband, Damon Laser, who said, "Yes, just do it, and we'll make it work," when I mentioned the idea of quitting my job to write a book about culture killers. Their consistent love and unwavering support through thick and thin enable me to conquer life's challenges and follow my heart.

I have been blessed with a large circle of family and friends, who continue to love and support me no matter how much I screw up. I love you all! I'd like to personal thank a few here who have made significant contributions and sacrifices to help me grow and develop. My parents, Dick and Earlene Bonin, for bringing me into this world and letting me experience life to the fullest. My grandparents, Lila and Earl "Flash" Williams, who taught me how to view life through different lenses and helped me develop a strong work ethic. Melissa Fisher, my sister from another mom and mister, whose message in "The Way of Hope" inspired me to follow my calling. Kayla Shiplette, for coming into my life and embracing me as her little sister. Dick Jr., Earl and Jon Paul Bonin, my younger brothers, for always being there for me when I need you and playing along with my many hairbrained ideas (remember Bonnish pepper?). Aunt Donna and Aunt Mary Alyce, for teaching me many important lessons through life. Dorothy Sims, for showing me the fruits (literally, peaches) of manual labor, and the value of perseverance. Pastor Joel Osteen and the Lakewood Church community, who continue to fill up my spiritual cup, inspire me to live in faith and never cast judgment.

I am extremely grateful for those who have mentored me along the way. Bob Pritchard, who opened doors of opportunity for me along my path. William Yaeger, who encouraged me to ask difficult questions and celebrate failures as opportunities to learn and grow stronger. Stuart Graudus, who recognized my potential and provided me with the knowledge and tools to expand my task-mastery into thought leadership. Chris Patton, a great mentor, friend and ally in impacting positive change. Mike Milicevic, who always had my back, even during the toughest of times.

If you've ever written a book, or prepared a presentation for an important meeting, you know it takes an army of people to pull it all together. This book series would still be a compilation of notebooks, sticky notes and bar napkins, if not for the efforts and dedication of so many others. I will forever be grateful to everyone who helped me organize my thoughts and translate my knowledge into something others could understand. My editor, Greg Brown, for not giving up on me when my obsession with getting it right slowed things down. Tom Zenner, for believing in me and helping me overcome a serious case of writer's block. Richele Theodore, for always being there when I need you and bending over backwards to make sure I ain't screwing up too badly! TAL Publishing, LLC for making it all look so easy. Everyone who reviewed drafts and provided valuable feedback, your light shone through the fog, helping me sculpt something special! The Hayzlett Group and TallGrass Public Relations, for believing in me and joining me on the journey towards impacting a more positive tomorrow.

There are far too many to mention, but I also want to thank everyone who has inspired, led and supported me throughout my life, including my coworkers, peers, leaders, mentors, professors, students, mentees and clients; classmates, ΣΣΣ sorority sisters, fellow members of the American Society of Safety Professionals (ASSP), book club ladies, friends and family.

For those of you who have assisted me on this journey and asked to remain anonymous, you know who you are -- thank you from the bottom of my heart! To maintain your anonymity, I've shared your stories from my perspective, and hope these books help you begin building a better path to success, both personally and within your organization.

Most importantly, I want to thank you, the reader, for joining me on this journey towards building a better path to a more positive future. I appreciate the conversations and correspondence with all my readers. Your engagement continues to introduce me to new perspectives and energize me to continue the journey, even when the road gets rough.

I hope this book and others in the Organization Culture Killers Deadly Practices series provide you with the knowledge and tools to impact positive change in your organizations, communities and personal life, and that you choose to share what you've learned with others.

In the revised wise words of Confucius, "The person ~~man~~ who moves a mountain begins by carrying away small stones."

As more people join our journey
to eradicate Deadly Practices
and build better paths to success,
the huge mountain standing
between us and 'better' will be
reduced to the gravel that paves
the way for future generations!

Definitions

CULTURE - An integrated pattern of human knowledge, belief, and behavior. In other words, the way people do things around here. Culture is something that is always present and shifts easily depending on the situation.

CULTURE OF SUCCESS - A culture that delivers performance in alignment with an organization's expectations and leadership.

CULTURE KILLERS - Even though a culture cannot physically be killed, the strongest culture can quickly become toxic. It can threaten an organization's ability to survive and thrive if Deadly Practices are introduced, which is why this book is titled "Organizational Culture Killers."

DEADLY PRACTICE (DP) – A destructive practice that hinders an organization's ability to achieve sustainable success.

EXPECTATIONS - The word expectation comes from the Latin word expectationem, meaning "an awaiting". In this book, expectations represent an organization's defined path to success as defined by leadership.

FOUNDATION - A body or ground upon which something is built up or overlaid, the basis of groundwork. In this book, the term Foundation refers to the organization's mission, vision, values and expectations set by leadership to support sustainable success of the organization.

FUCKUS - To increase risks in the organization when too much 'focus' is placed on something without considering the impact it will have in other areas and ensuring balance between the three P's.

97

INDICATORS - Statistical values to measure current conditions as well as forecast trends and outcomes.

KEY PERFORMANCE INDICATOR (KPI) - A measurable value that demonstrates the delivery effectiveness of an organization's expectations. When applied thoughtfully, KPIs can provide insights into the future and add visibility to trends by quantifying current conditions.

LAGGING INDICATOR - A measurement that quantifies current conditions and confirms occurring patterns. It is typically "output" oriented, follows an event, and is easy to measure but hard to improve or influence.

LEADING INDICATOR - A measurement that provides insight into the future. It requires an in-depth understanding of the organization's risks along with the specific controls needed to prevent a risk event from occurring, so it is easy to influence but difficult to measure.

LEARNINGS - An organization's ability to recognize opportunities for continuous improvement from both internal and external successes and failures. Learnings can result from experimentation, experiences, observations, investigations, analysis, benchmarking, word-of-mouth, and various other sources.

MISSION - How an organization differentiates itself from others and what its path to success will entail.

OPERATING AND PERFORMANCE ALL-INCLUSIVE LEADERSHIP SYSTEM (OPALS) – A comprehensive system that defines how an organization delivers success in alignment with its expectations. This varies from a management system in that it includes expectations for leaders of an organization along with criteria for performance.

ORGANIZATION - In this book, the term organization is used to represent entities of any size, demographic, or geographic location where people work together to achieve success. These include, but are not limited to: agencies, businesses, corporations, non-for-profits, sports teams, schools, start-ups, families, etc.

PERFORMANCE - A term used to express of how well an organization executes its expectations for success.

PRACTICE - The way in which work is usually done in an organization.

REQUIREMENT - That which is required; a thing demanded or obligatory. In this book requirements include, but are not limited to, written and implied: regulations, laws, mandates, policies, procedures, practices, processes and rules that have been defined or accepted as actions necessary to deliver sustainable success in alignment with the organization's expectations.

SILO - When separation of an organization's employees occurs due to differences (e.g.: department, skills, teams, etc.).

SUCCESS – This one's a bit tricky to define since success can mean many different things to everyone. The term success originated in the Mid-16th century from Latin *successus*, from the verb succedere, meaning to "come close after" and historically has been defined as the good or bad outcome of an undertaking. If you conduct an online search for the term "success" on the Internet of Things (IoT) dozens of different definitions will pop up, ranging from simply being happy to world domination. For this book, success is defined as an organization's ability to meet its market's demands in alignment with its mission, vision, and expectations.

THE JOURNEY - In this book, the journey refers to the worldwide initiative needed to impact positive changes with regards to how organizations view, attain and maintain success, simply stated "How Leaders Build Cultures of Success". The methods being used currently are counterproductive and ultimately flawed. It's time to stop repeating the mistakes of our past and start building better paths to success!

VALUES - Important and lasting beliefs or ideals shared by the members of a culture about what is good or bad and desirable or undesirable. Values have a major influence on behavior and attitude and serve as broad guidelines in all situations. Some common business values are fairness, innovation and community involvement.

VISION - An organization's overarching aspirations of what it hopes to achieve or to become in the future.

Index

101

Reflections and Commitments

1. Use the following "Reflections and Commitments" pages to document the things you learned from this book, responses to the reflection questions at the end of each chapter and the actions you are committed to act upon/delegate to begin building a better path to success.

2. Next, set a recurring reminder on your calendar to revisit these reflections, confirm progress, and make updates as necessary.

3. I would love to learn more about your journey and assist you in any way I can, so please contact me if you would like to share your experiences, ask questions, or collaborate on future books.

BEST OF LUCK!

Your Reflections and Commitments

Your Reflections and Commitments

Your Reflections and Commitments

Your Reflections and Commitments

Your Reflections and Commitments

Your Reflections and Commitments

Your Reflections and Commitments

Your Reflections and Commitments

Your Reflections and Commitments

Your Reflections and Commitments

Invitation for Review

My desire for learning is endless, so I would love to hear from you. What did you like? What do you want more of? What worked and what didn't? You don't have to worry about hurting my feelings or damaging my pride. I practice what I teach, frequently search my reflection for cracks and celebrate their discovery as opportunities to improve. I'm far from perfect but grow stronger every day through self-reflection and the honesty of others. Please visit **www.talaser.com** to:

- Access resources discussed in this book.

- Discussed questions or need assistance with any of the Deadly Practices, solutions or tools referenced in this book.

- Share your personal experiences and learnings to help add value to future books and communications.

- Schedule OPALS gap assessments, culture assessments, leadership coaching, workshops, keynote or other consultation needs.

- Receive information on book bulk discount pricing.

- Subscribe to T.A. Laser's mailing list to:
    - Receive learning alerts.
    - Be notified when resources and tools are added.
    - Receive book release and signing event updates.

9 781732 829916